Margaret Knight
and the Paper Bag

By Virginia Loh-Hagan

Published in the United States of America by
Cherry Lake Publishing
Ann Arbor, Michigan
www.cherrylakepublishing.com

Content Adviser: Kirsten Edwards, MA, Educational Studies
Reading Adviser: Marla Conn, MS, Ed., Literacy specialist, Read-Ability, Inc.

Photo Credits: © jannoon028/Shutterstock.com, Cover, 1; © Vibe Images/Shutterstock.com, 4; © Pictures From History/
Newscom, 6; © Rawpixel.com/Shutterstock.com, 8; © ArnoldReinhold/Wikimedia Commons, 10; © Dean Drobot/
Shutterstock.com, 12; © sirtravelalot/Shutterstock.com, 14; © Margaret Knight (US220925)/United States Patent and
Trademark Office/www.uspto.gov, 16; © Everett Historical/Shutterstock.com, 18; © wavebreakmedia/Shutterstock.com, 20

Library of Congress Cataloging-in-Publication Data

Names: Loh-Hagan, Virginia, author.
Title: Margaret Knight and the paper bag / by Virginia Loh-Hagan.
Description: Ann Arbor : Cherry Lake Publishing, [2018] | Series: Women innovators |
    Includes bibliographical references and index. | Audience: Grades 4 to 6.
Identifiers: LCCN 2018003304| ISBN 9781534129139 (hardcover) | ISBN 9781534132337 (pbk.) |
    ISBN 9781534130838 (pdf) | ISBN 9781534134034 (hosted ebook)
Subjects: LCSH: Knight, Margaret E., 1838-1914–Juvenile literature. | Inventors–United States–Biography–Juvenile literature. |
    Women inventors–United States–Biography–Juvenile literature. | Paper bags–Juvenile literature.
Classification: LCC T40.K55 L64 2018 | DDC 676/.33092 [B] –dc23
LC record available at https://lccn.loc.gov/2018003304

Cherry Lake Publishing would like to acknowledge the work of The Partnership for 21st Century Skills.
Please visit *www.p21.org* for more information.

Printed in the United States of America
Corporate Graphics

CONTENTS

Recycle or reuse paper bags in a creative way.
It's fun and helps save the environment.

A Woman

How often do you think about paper bags? You probably don't. But you use them all the time. Paper bags are everywhere. Bags make it easy for people to carry things from one place to another.

There are many reasons why people use paper bags. When people shop, they need to put their things somewhere. They can choose a paper or plastic bag. People also put their lunches in brown paper bags.

Knight's nickname was Mattie.

Margaret Knight invented the paper bags we know today. She was an American inventor.

Knight was born on February 14, 1838, in Maine. After her father died, her family moved to New Hampshire. She only went to school for a few years before she had to drop out. Knight had to help take care

Look!

Look around the house. Look for problems to fix. Invent something to solve the problem.

Inventors go through many phases of trial and error.

of her **siblings** and make money. She went to work at a cotton **mill**.

She saw an accident at the cotton mill. A worker was hurt by one of the mill's machines. At only 12 years old, Knight invented a safety **device** to stop future accidents. Her bosses at the mill liked her invention so much that they used it.

She was always **tinkering**. She built toys for her brothers. She made a foot warmer for her mother. She fixed problems she saw around the house. She used whatever tools and materials were available.

Machines help make work easier and faster.

An Idea

Knight left the mill because of health problems. She took a job at the Columbia Paper Bag Company. She found problems to fix there, too. She thought it would be easier to pack things in bags if they had flat bottoms. She also thought it took too long to make bags by hand.

Inventors sketch out their ideas.

She drew plans and built a model out of wood. Her machine folded and glued paper to form flat-bottomed brown paper bags. It made over 1,000 bags in a short amount of time.

Workers weren't sure about Knight's machine. They doubted women could invent useful things. Knight didn't quit. She went to a local shop and worked with a **machinist**. She made a model out of iron. She kept improving it. She worked with more machinists.

She applied for a **patent**. But to her surprise, someone else had already filed for one. Charles Annan had stolen Knight's

Courts make decisions about the law.

idea. Annan was one of the machinists who worked with Knight.

Knight fought back. She took Annan to court. She said the patent was hers. Annan said a woman was not capable of inventing such an **innovative** machine. Knight showed proof, sharing her drawings and models. She won the patent in 1871.

Make a Guess!

Get paper bags of different sizes. How many items can you fit into each bag? Make a guess!

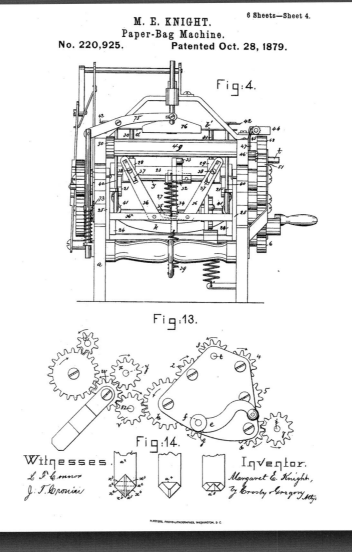

Today, thousands of machines based on Knight's ideas are in use around the world.

A Legacy

Knight was more than an inventor. She was also a businesswoman. After making the machine, she formed the Eastern Paper Bag Company. Her **legacy** can be seen in how she changed our daily lives.

Before Knight's invention, shoppers carried items in wooden crates or in paper cones. Paper bags were more like envelopes. This wasn't very handy. Knight's

Newspapers compared her to Thomas Edison.

paper bags made life easier. Her bags are used around the world.

Women were not treated fairly during Knight's lifetime. They were not taken seriously. Knight showed the world that women could be inventors. She filed over 20 patents and created over 100 inventions.

She invented all types of things. She made a machine that cut the soles of shoes. She made a shield for dresses and skirts. It helped protect the clothing against rain, snow, and mud. She made special **engines**. She loved inventing machines and tools.

The best inventions solve simple problems.

Knight was given several awards. England's Queen Victoria recognized her in 1871. She was honored in the National Inventors Hall of Fame in 2006. Her **original** bag-making machine is at the Smithsonian Museum in Washington, D.C.

Knight died on October 12, 1914. Think of her the next time you pick up a flat-bottomed paper bag.

Think!

Think about some inventors. Compare male and female inventors. Why would it be harder for female inventors to get noticed?

GLOSSARY

device (dih-VISE) a piece of equipment that does a particular job

engines (EN-juhnz) machines with moving parts that convert power into motion

innovative (IN-uh-vay-tiv) describing something that introduces a new idea or invention

legacy (LEG-uh-see) something handed down from one generation to another

machinist (muh-SHEE-nist) a person who makes, uses, or fixes a machine

mill (MIL) a factory that produces fabrics and other processed materials

original (uh-RIJ-uh-nuhl) first or earliest version

patent (PAT-uhnt) the right from the government to use or sell an invention for a certain number of years

siblings (SIB-lingz) brothers or sisters

tinkering (TING-ker-ing) the act of trying to fix or make something

FIND OUT MORE

BOOKS

Kulling, Monica. *In the Bag! Margaret Knight Wraps It Up!* Toronto: Tundra Books, 2011.

McCully, Emily Arnold. *Marvelous Mattie! How Margaret E. Knight Became an Inventor*. New York: Farrar, Straus, and Giroux, 2006.

Thimmesh, Catherine. *Girls Think of Everything: Stories of Ingenious Inventions by Women*. Boston: Houghton Mifflin Company, 2000.

WEBSITES

Famous Women Inventors—Margaret Knight: Invention of the Paper Bag Machine
www.women-inventors.com/Margaret-Knight.asp
Read a brief biography about Knight's life and achievements.

Medium—Timeline: Thank Inventor Margaret E. Knight for the Modern Marvel That Is the Paper Bag
https://timeline.com/margaret-e-knight-paper-bag-f5d474c0f3d2
Learn more about Knight's life.

INDEX

ABOUT THE AUTHOR

Dr. Virginia Loh-Hagan is an author, university professor, former classroom teacher, and curriculum designer. She always chooses paper bags over plastic bags. She lives in San Diego with her very tall husband and very naughty dogs. To learn more about her, visit www.virginialoh.com.